11/12

P9-BIL-733

Levers

BY KATIE MARSICO • ILLUSTRATED BY REGINALD BUTLER

The Child's World®

Published by The Child's World®
1980 Lookout Drive • Mankato, MN 56003-1705
800-599-READ • www.childsworld.com

Acknowledgments
The Child's World®: Mary Berendes, Publishing Director
The Design Lab: Cover and interior design
Amnet: Cover and interior production
Red Line Editorial: Editorial direction

Photo credits
Roman Milert/iStockphoto, cover, 1; Shutterstock Images, 7;
Sergey Lavrentev/Shutterstock Images, 9; Rob Cruse/
iStockphoto, 12; Alexander Raths/Shutterstock Images, 16;
Nicholas Moore/Shutterstock Images, 20; iStockphoto, 23

Design Elements: In.light/Dreamstime

Copyright © 2013 by The Child's World®
All rights reserved. No part of this book may be
reproduced or utilized in any form or by any means
without written permission from the publisher.

ISBN 9781614732747
LCCN 2012933653

Printed in the United States of America
Mankato, MN
July 2012
PA02120

ABOUT THE AUTHOR

Katie Marsico is the author of more than 100 children's and young-adult reference books. She enjoys using levers to cook, garden, and do crafts.

ABOUT THE ILLUSTRATOR

Reginald Butler is a professional artist whose work includes poetry, painting, design, animation, commercial graphics, and music. One day he hopes to wake up and read his comic in the paper while watching his cartoon on television.

Table of Contents

Tools and Machines

What would your life be like without tools and machines? You use tools and machines every day. Tools and machines help you do **work**. Computers are machines that help you store information. Cars are machines that help you move from place to place. Washing machines help you clean your clothes. These kinds of machines have many moving parts. Machines with many moving parts are **complex**. Complex machines are made up of many simple machines. There are six types of simple machines. They are levers, inclined planes, wedges, screws, wheels, and pulleys. It's time to find out about levers. Get ready to learn a load about lifting and lowering!

Simple machines make working in the yard easier.

Lifting, Lowering, and Opening

A lever is made up of two main parts. The first piece is a handle, bar, or stick. This is called the lever arm. The arm turns on a fixed point called the **fulcrum**. You use a lever to move a heavy load. You can also use a lever to open something. One end of the arm raises or lowers an object when you push or pull on the other end.

A seesaw is an example of a lever. Your weight lowers one end of the seesaw when you sit down. Your friend's side of the seesaw lifts up.

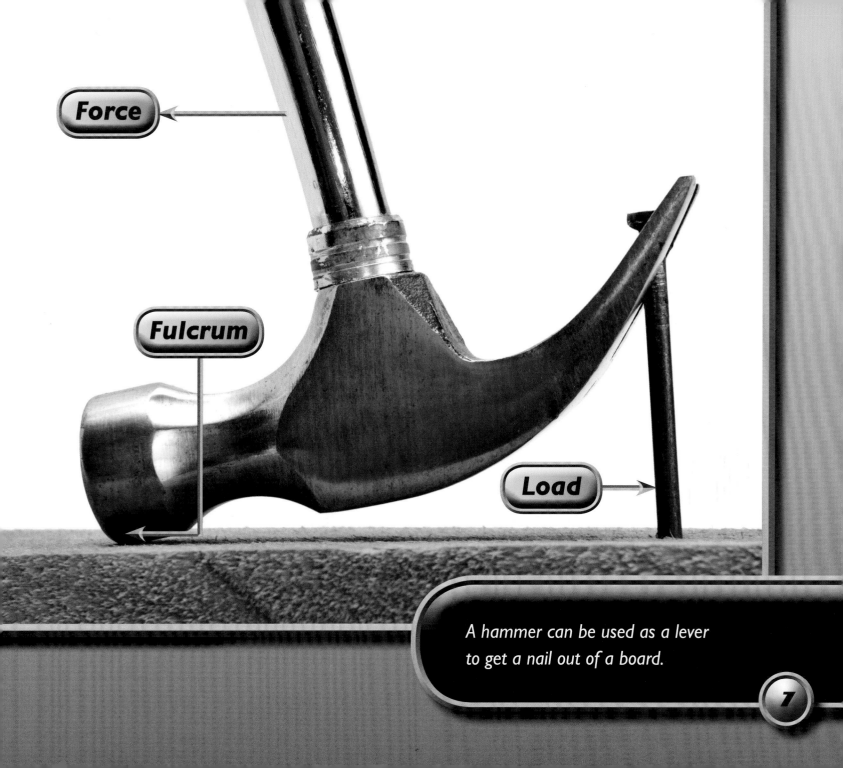

Force

Fulcrum

Load

A hammer can be used as a lever
to get a nail out of a board.

Same Task, Less Effort

How do levers make work easier? Look at the seesaw example. It is pretty easy to lift your friend. You just sit down on the seesaw, and he pushes off the ground a bit. But imagine if you had to lift your friend without the seesaw. Would it be harder? You bet! Without the lever you would have to use more **effort** to lift your friend. A lever lets you do a task with less effort than you would use without the lever.

A seesaw is a fun way to use a lever.

From Seesawing to Paint-Opening

There are three types of levers. The first type is called a first-class lever. Seesaws and paint openers are first-class levers. The fulcrum is between where the load sits and the part of the arm you push or pull.

SIMPLE TOOLS FOR SEA OTTERS

People are not the only ones who use levers. Some animals have also figured out how useful these machines can be. Sea otters use rocks to **pry** open seashells. The otters then eat the sea urchins or sea snails that live inside.

You can keep a friend raised in the air easily on a seesaw.

Load

Force

Fulcrum

A *flathead screwdriver is the lever that forces the paint can's lid off.*

Have you ever opened a can of paint? Ask your parents if you have a paint can at home that you can open. You can use a paint opener or a flathead screwdriver. Place the flat end of the lever under the lip of the paint lid. The lid is the load. Then push the lever arm down so it turns on the paint can's edge. The edge is the fulcrum. Using this type of lever makes it easier to pry something open that is shut. A crowbar is also a first-class lever.

Work That Wheelbarrow

The second type of lever is a second-class lever.
Nutcrackers and wheelbarrows are second-class levers.
(Nutcrackers are actually two levers put together.)
The load rests between the fulcrum and the part of the
arm you push or pull.

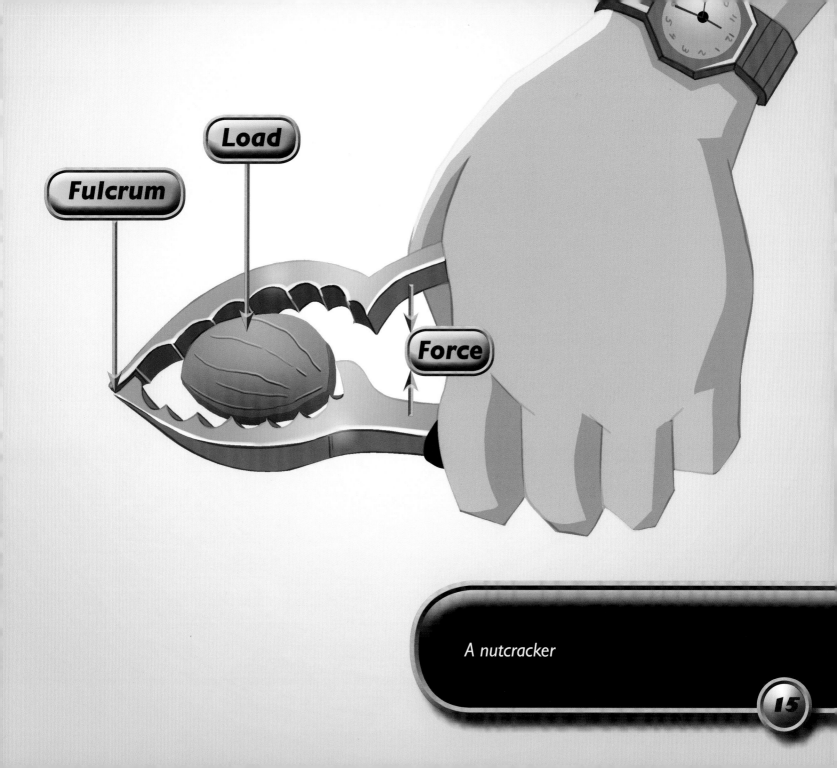

Fulcrum

Load

Force

A nutcracker

15

Force

Load

Fulcrum

Using a wheelbarrow to move a bunch of flowers is easier than carrying them by hand.

Imagine you are gardening with your dad. You have a pile of dirt you need to move into the garden. How can you get it there with the least amount of effort?

By using a wheelbarrow! You pull up the handles. These are the arms of the lever. The wheel is the fulcrum. The dirt, or load, sits between the handles and the wheel.

Your Body's Levers

The final type of lever is a third-class lever. Brooms, shovels, and even your own arms are third-class levers. The fulcrum is on one end of this lever. The load you are raising or lowering is on the other end.

Fulcrum

Force

Load

When you shovel, you are using a third-class lever.

Load

Fulcrum

Force

A baseball player uses a third-class lever to hit a baseball.

Lift a glass of water off the table by bending at the elbow. Your elbow is the fulcrum. You use the lower part of your arm to place an upward force on the glass. The glass is the load you are moving.

BATTER UP!

Have you ever swung a bat to hit a baseball? You were actually swinging a third-class lever! Your elbows were the fulcrum. You used your arms and hands to apply force. The bat was the load. You used less effort to get the ball farther than you could have just by throwing it.

Levers Everywhere

Now you know about levers. These simple machines are everywhere! They are in your backyard and on your body. Levers help you on the playground. They make it easier to raise and lower objects. These simple machines have changed the world. How will you use levers today?

Load

Force

Fulcrum

When you lift a glass to take a drink, your arm is acting as a lever.

GLOSSARY

complex (kuhm-PLEKS): If something is complex, it has a lot of parts. A computer is a complex machine.

effort (EF-urt): Effort is the amount of force that must be used to do work. It takes less effort to use a lever than to do the same task without a lever.

fulcrum (FUL-kruhm): A fulcrum is the fixed point on which a lever turns. On a wheelbarrow, the fulcrum is the wheel.

pry (PRYE): If people pry, they raise or pull apart things by applying forces. Paint openers are used to pry open paint cans.

work (WURK): Work is applying a force, such as pulling or pushing, to move an object. You do work when you lift your friend up on a seesaw.

BOOKS

Arnold, Nick. *How Machines Work: The Interactive Guide to Simple Machines and Mechanisms*. Philadelphia, PA: Running Press, 2011.

Bodden, Valerie. *Levers*. Mankato, MN: Creative Education, 2011.

Gosman, Gillian. *Levers in Action*. New York: PowerKids Press, 2011.

WEB SITES

Visit our Web site for links about levers:
childsworld.com/links

Note to Parents, Teachers, and Librarians: We routinely verify our Web links to make sure they are safe and active sites. So encourage your readers to check them out!

INDEX